Pattern-Driven
Software Problem Solving
Introduction

Dmitry Vostokov
Memory Dump Analysis Services

Published by OpenTask, Republic of Ireland

OpenTask books and magazines are available through booksellers and distributors worldwide. For further information or comments send requests to press@opentask.com.

A CIP catalog record for this book is available from the British Library.

ISBN-l3: 978-1-908043-17-7 (Paperback)

First printing, 2011

Revision 2.1 (May, 2015)

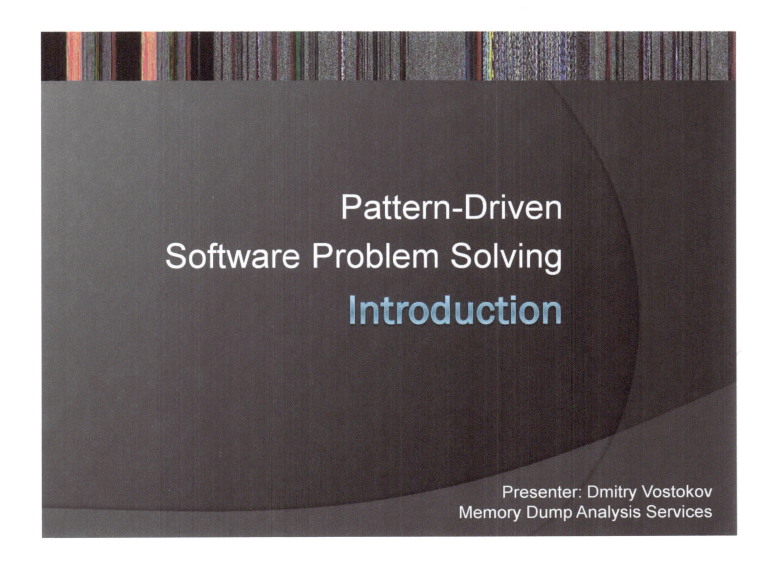

Hello, Everyone! My name is Dmitry Vostokov, and I'm a founder of Memory Dump Analysis Services which specializes in crash dump analysis and debugging. The topic of today's presentation is Software Problem Solving using patterns. The topic is so big that I devised a whole series of such presentations with this particular one being just an introduction.

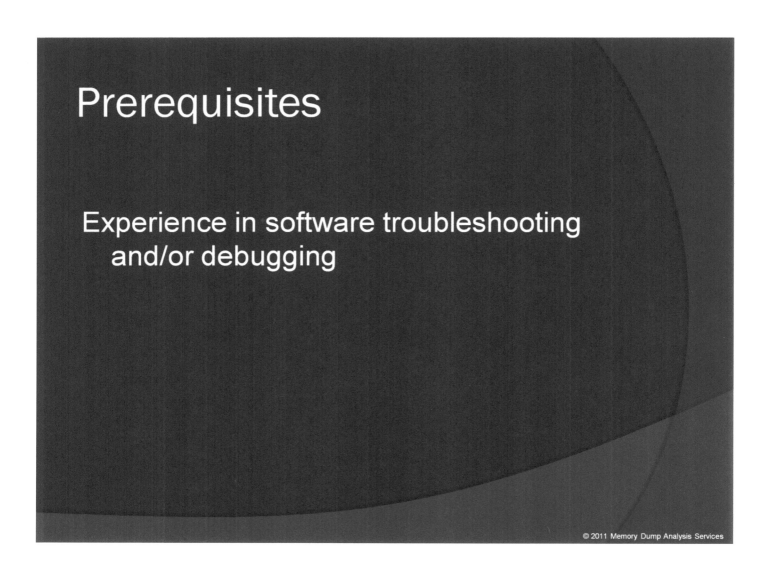

I assume that you already have some experience in software troubleshooting or debugging. There is something for everyone in this presentation even if you have never fixed any software defect.

Agenda (Summary)

- A Short History
- Basic Definitions
- Pattern Categories
- Future Research Directions

This is a short presentation. Instead of trying to cover everything about patterns I only provide hints and links where to find further information. I survey what I have done during the last 5 years. Because ...

DumpAnalysis.org*

5 Years!

... tomorrow is 5 years of DumpAnalysis.org. Originally conceived as a forum to discuss memory dump analysis issues it was later transformed into a blog, then into a portal, then it was a dream to become ForensicAnalysis.org, and then it became associated with software trace analysis via TraceAnalysis.org and finally with Victimware.org.

Agenda (Basic Definitions)

- Software Problems
- Software Patterns
- DA+TA
- Pattern Hybridization

First we talk about software problems and clarify which problem category we consider for this presentation. Next we talk about software patterns and also clarify which pattern category we consider here. Then we have a look at **DA+TA** acronym and define a metaphor we call **Pattern Hybridization**.

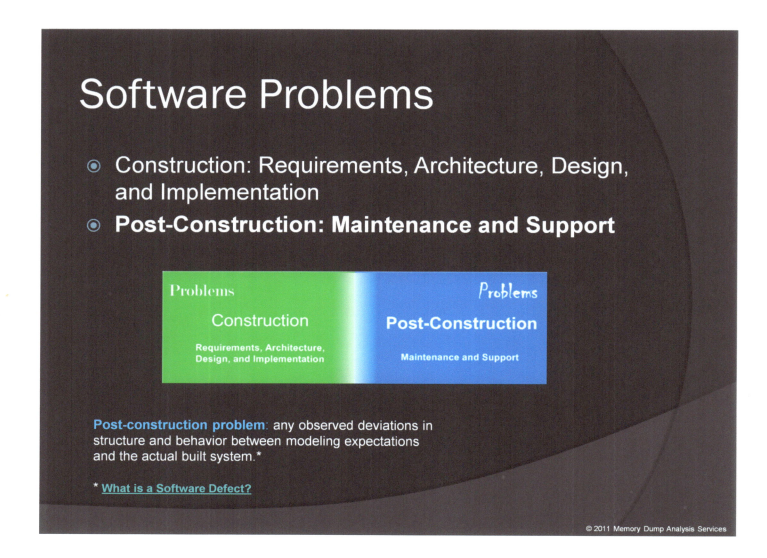

What is a Software Defect?

http://www.dumpanalysis.org/blog/index.php/2008/01/08/what-is-a-software-defect/

Let's consider software problems. Software development engineers usually think about software problems as problems with building software (construction problems), for example, design problems. Software support engineers usually think about software problems as problems in production environments (we call it post-construction problems). The distinction is not clear-cut, and there is some overlap between these two categories. The typical construction example: "How we design and build a system based on functional requirements and non-functional constraints?" The typical post-construction example: "What we had built stopped working. How do we bring it back working?"

Software Patterns

- Construction: Requirements, Architecture, Design, and Implementation
- **Post-Construction: Maintenance and Support**

Pattern: a common recurrent identifiable problem together with a set of recommendations and possible solutions to apply in a specific context

We use patterns to solve problems. Here we relax the usual definition of a pattern having a definite solution. Anything works. So our definition is this: a common recurrent identifiable problem together with a set of recommendations and possible solutions to apply in a specific context. Patterns are also a part of pattern language useful for communication. Again our main focus is on post-construction patterns although we consider construction patterns for troubleshooting and debugging tools.

DA+TA

⊙ DA: Dump Artifact / Dump Analysis

Memory snapshots: process, kernel, physical memory dumps

⊙ TA: Trace Artifact / Trace Analysis

Software traces: Event Tracing for Windows, logs

© 2011 Memory Dump Analysis Services

By chance, **DATA** looks like a good abbreviation for **D**ump **A**rtifact **A**nalysis and **T**race **A**rtifact **A**nalysis. By a dump we mean a memory snapshot usually called memory dump, crash dump, or core dump. By a trace, we mean a log, for example, Process Monitor logs or Citrix CDF traces which are based on Microsoft Event Tracing for Windows.

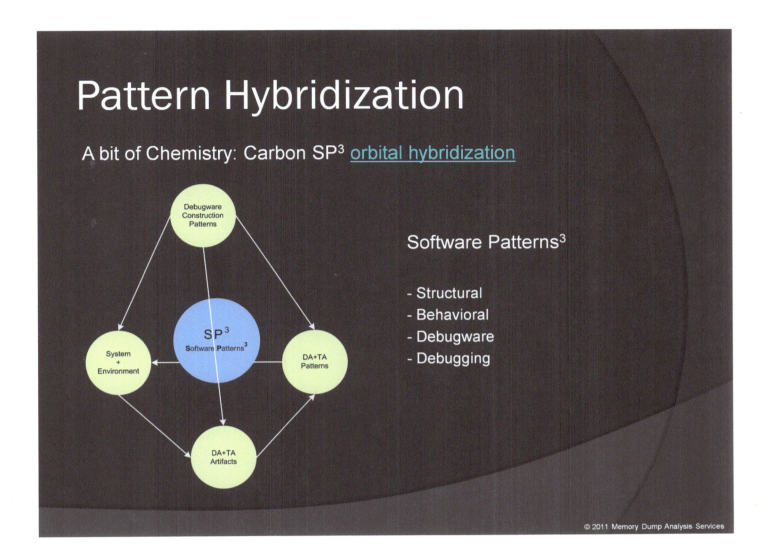

Orbital hybridization

http://en.wikipedia.org/wiki/Orbital_hybridisation

Now we introduce Pattern Hybridization. This is just a fancy term borrowed from Chemistry with an acronym **SP3** to name the mixture of 4 types of **S**oftware **P**atterns: Structural, Behavioral, Tools, and Debugging. The diagram shows the pattern-driven process where a system and its environment provide DATA artifacts which we analyze and recognize DATA patterns in them. The results are used to alter the system and its environment. All these stages are facilitated by patterns for troubleshooting and debugging tools which we call **Debugware** patterns. Tools are used to produce and collect artifacts, alter the system and its environment, and to recognize other patterns.

Agenda (Pattern Categories)

- Software Behavior
- Debugware Tools
- Problem Workaround
- Unified Debugging

Now we come to the next block of slides. We consider pattern categories such as Software Behavior, Debugware, Workaround, and Unified Debugging.

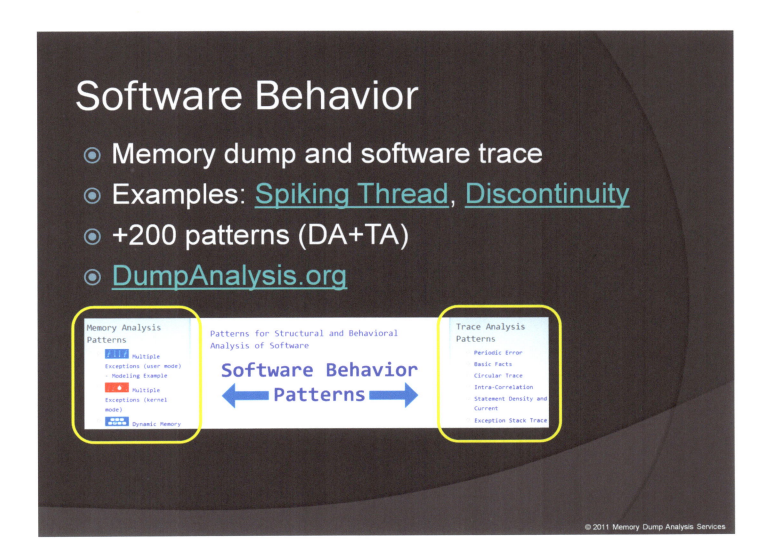

Spiking Thread
http://www.dumpanalysis.org/blog/index.php/2007/05/11/crash-dump-analysis-patterns-part-14/

Discontinuity
http://www.dumpanalysis.org/blog/index.php/2009/08/04/trace-analysis-patterns-part-8/

Software behavior patterns are visible and discernible signs in memory dump and software trace artifacts as a result of the analysis. Some of them are results from software defects, and some are results from unanticipated and unexpected software interaction. There are lots of patterns on DumpAnalysis.org portal. The picture shows that when you go there on the left-hand side you would see memory dump analysis patterns and on the right-hand side you would see software trace analysis patterns. You may notice some pictures or icons on the left: this is a not yet completed project to give each pattern a pattern icon. When we finish with dump analysis patterns, you would see icons on the right too.

DA: Software Behavior

- Memory dump: a memory snapshot
- Definition, partial classification and historical list
- Pattern identification case studies

Definition, partial classification and historical list
http://www.dumpanalysis.org/blog/index.php/crash-dump-analysis-patterns/

Pattern identification case studies
http://www.dumpanalysis.org/blog/index.php/pattern-cooperation/

This slide provides various links to memory dump analysis patterns and their case studies that you can browse when you download the presentation PDF file afterward from this location:

http://www.patterndiagnostics.com/files/Pattern-Driven-Software-Problem-Solving-Introduction.pdf

TA: Software Behavior

"Imagine you got a software trace from hundreds of modules you haven't written or haven't seen source code of..."

- Software trace: a sequence of memory fragments ordered in time
- Definition, and historical list
- Pattern identification case studies

© 2011 Memory Dump Analysis Services

Definition, and historical list

http://www.dumpanalysis.org/blog/index.php/trace-analysis-patterns/

Pattern identification case studies

http://www.dumpanalysis.org/blog/index.php/pattern-cooperation/

Similar links are available for software trace analysis patterns and their case studies. Actually there are parallels between some software trace patterns and memory dump patterns. For example, stack traces can be analyzed using some trace analysis patterns. The patterns we propose are general and not tied to a specific product. Because I used to analyze software traces with millions of lines and with messages from hundreds of components where most of them were completely unfamiliar for me (and I had never seen underlying source code) I proposed very general ones that can be used even for network traces.

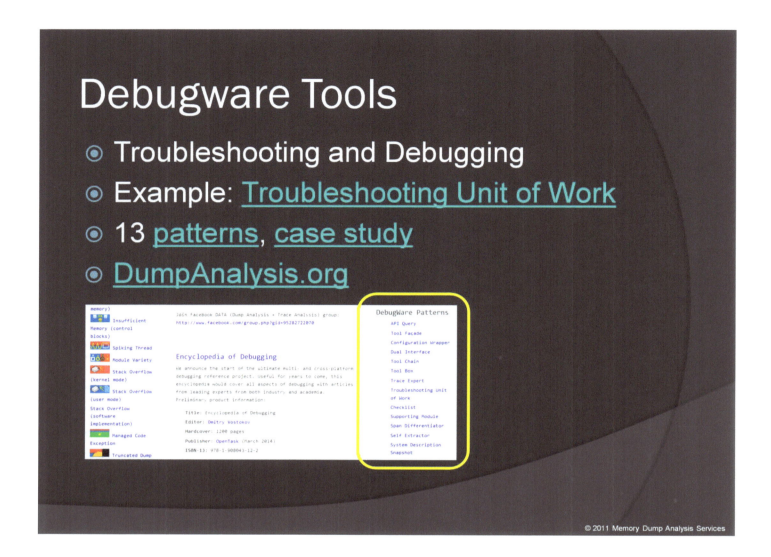

Troubleshooting Unit of Work

http://www.dumpanalysis.org/blog/index.php/2009/09/21/debugware-patterns-part-8/

Patterns

http://www.dumpanalysis.org/blog/index.php/debugware-patterns/

Case study

http://www.dumpanalysis.org/blog/index.php/2009/10/30/debugware-patterns-a-case-study-part-1/

Now we provide links to Debugware patterns. There are not so many of them now but more will be coming in the future. One example is **TUW**, **T**roubleshooting **U**nit of **W**ork, where a certain troubleshooting action or a set of actions is factored out into a separate module. If you visit Dump Analysis Portal and scroll its main page, you would see Debugware patterns on the right-hand side after the trace analysis pattern list.

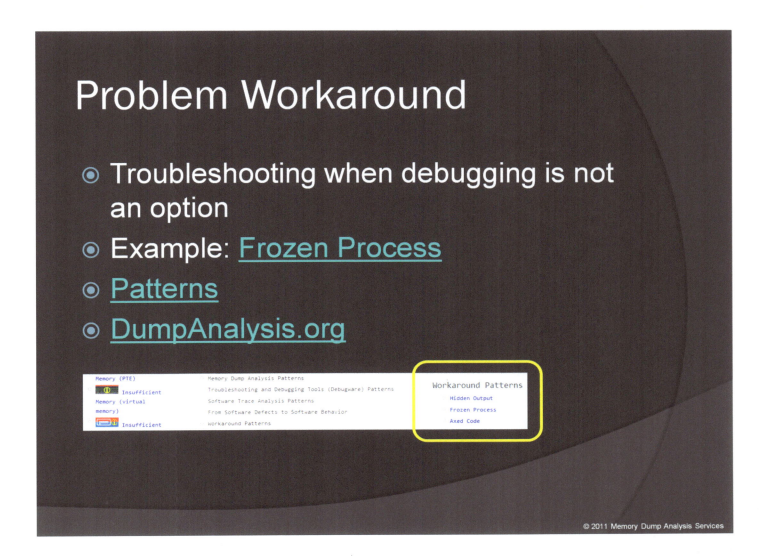

Frozen Process

http://www.dumpanalysis.org/blog/index.php/2010/01/25/workaround-patterns-part-2/

Patterns

http://www.dumpanalysis.org/blog/index.php/workaround-patterns/

Not all post-construction problems are amenable to fixes, especially if there are time and resource constraints. In such cases, we can use Workaround patterns to provide temporary solutions. For example, **Axing Code** instead of modifying a specific line or freezing a process or removing conflicting applications. There is much work here to expand the pattern list.

Unified Debugging

- Systematic Pattern Language
- Example:

Analysis Patterns	*Shared Buffer Overwrite*
Architectural Patterns	*Debug Event Subscription / Notification*
Design Patterns	*Punctuated Execution*
Implementation Patterns	*Breakpoint (software and hardware)*
Usage Patterns	*Kernel vs. user space breakpoints*

© 2011 Memory Dump Analysis Services

Shared Buffer Overwrite

http://www.dumpanalysis.org/blog/index.php/2010/10/18/crash-dump-analysis-patterns-part-110/

We also started the unification of software behavior analysis patterns with debugging architecture, design, implementation, and usage. This is analogous to software construction where a problem analysis leads to various software engineering phases. The important difference here is the addition of debugging usage patterns, for example, kernel vs. user space breakpoints. To differentiate this systematic approach from the various published ad hoc debugging patterns we call it **Unified Debugging Pattern Language**. Architecture, design, and implementation parts can also correspond to various Debugware patterns.

Agenda (Future Directions)

- Structural Memory Patterns
- Unified Debugging Pattern Language
- Domain Pattern Hierarchy
- Periodic Table of Software Defects

The last section is about future directions (what to expect in the nearest future).

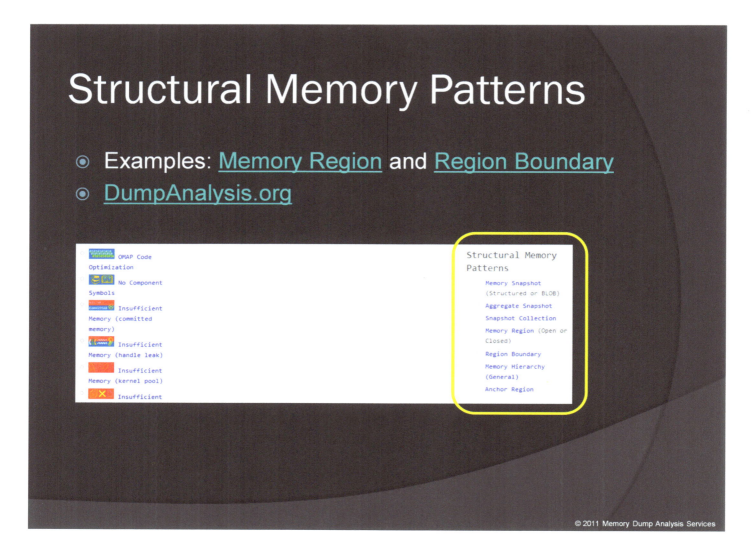

Memory Region

http://www.dumpanalysis.org/blog/index.php/2010/10/01/structural-memory-patterns-part-4/

Region Boundary

http://www.dumpanalysis.org/blog/index.php/2010/10/01/structural-memory-patterns-part-5/

We can divide memory and trace analysis patterns mostly seen as abnormal software behavior into behavioral and structural catalogs. The goal is to account for normal system-independent structural entities and relationships visible in memory like modules, threads, processes, etc. For example, one such pattern (and also a super pattern) is called **Memory Snapshot**. It is further subdivided into **Structured Memory Snapshot** and **BLOB Memory Snapshot.** Structured sub-pattern includes:

- Contiguous memory dump files with artificially generated headers (for example, physical or process virtual space memory dump)
- Software trace messages with imposed internal structure

BLOB sub-pattern variety includes address range snapshots without any externally imposed structure, for example, saved by *.writemem* WinDbg command or *ReadProcessMemory* Win32 API and contiguous buffer and raw memory dumps saved by various memory acquisition tools.

Behavioral patterns that relate to Memory Snapshot pattern are:

False Positive Dump

http://www.dumpanalysis.org/blog/index.php/2006/11/01/crash-dump-analysis-patterns-part-3/

Lateral Damage

http://www.dumpanalysis.org/blog/index.php/2006/11/03/crash-dump-analysis-patterns-part-4/

Inconsistent Dump

http://www.dumpanalysis.org/blog/index.php/2007/01/24/crash-dump-analysis-patterns-part-7/

Truncated Dump

http://www.dumpanalysis.org/blog/index.php/2007/07/20/crash-dump-analysis-patterns-part-18/

Early Crash Dump

http://www.dumpanalysis.org/blog/index.php/2007/11/21/crash-dump-analysis-patterns-part-37/

Manual Dump (kernel)

http://www.dumpanalysis.org/blog/index.php/2007/12/12/crash-dump-analysis-patterns-part-41a/

Manual Dump (process)

http://www.dumpanalysis.org/blog/index.php/2007/12/17/crash-dump-analysis-patterns-part-41b/

Corrupt Dump

http://www.dumpanalysis.org/blog/index.php/2008/01/24/crash-dump-analysis-patterns-part-43/

No Process Dumps

http://www.dumpanalysis.org/blog/index.php/2008/01/30/crash-dump-analysis-patterns-part-45/

No System Dumps

http://www.dumpanalysis.org/blog/index.php/2008/01/31/crash-dump-analysis-patterns-part-46/

Self-Dump

http://www.dumpanalysis.org/blog/index.php/2008/02/22/crash-dump-analysis-patterns-part-52/

Abridged Dump

http://www.dumpanalysis.org/blog/index.php/2010/08/04/crash-dump-analysis-patterns-part-104/

Other examples include **Memory Region** and **Region Boundary** such as a stack and its guard page.

Domain Pattern Hierarchy

Repeated patterns through the layers of software

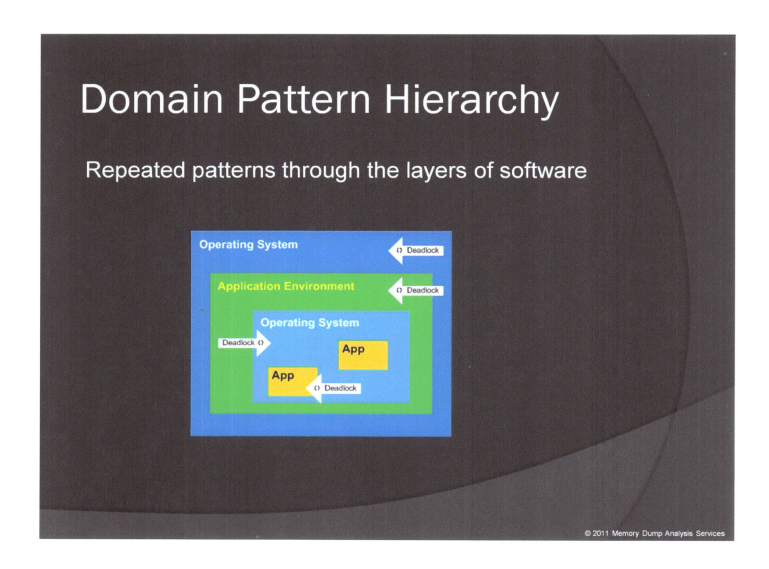

Next I'm working at is the so-called domain pattern hierarchy where we have the same repeated patterns through software layers such as virtualization. For example, an OS can have managed or interpreted code environment (such as .NET and Java) with another OS implemented in .NET language and Java (as a research project, for example), the latter OS can have its own Apps written in the same or completely different language. As you can see, a deadlock is possible in every layer although pattern internals would be different in each case.

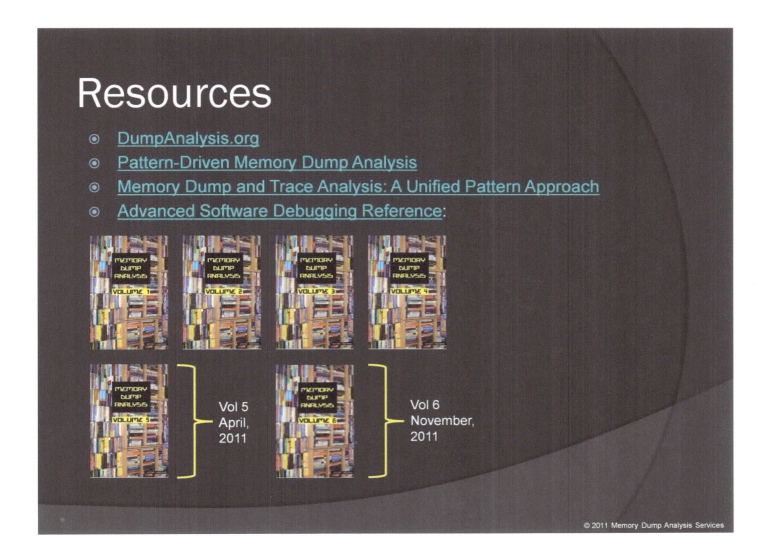

Memory Dump and Trace Analysis: A Unified Pattern Approach

http://www.debuggingexperts.com/memory-dump-trace-analysis-unified-pattern-approach

Advanced Software Debugging Reference

http://www.dumpanalysis.org/advanced-software-debugging-reference

This slide has links for further study including a presentation with full transcript comments about pattern-driven memory dump analysis I delivered 2 years ago and a full case study from Debugging Experts Magazine.

Note: I was planning to release volume 5 before this presentation but I couldn't. Should be published by the end of this month or in early April. Volume 6 is scheduled by the end of this year.

www.ingramcontent.com/pod-product-compliance
Lightning Source LLC
LaVergne TN
LVHW071524070326
832902LV00003B/72